MVP

MEMORY VERSE & PRAYER

Journal

APPLY THE WRITTEN

Word of God

TO YOUR PRAYERS

MVP

MEMORY VERSE & PRAYER

Journal

FERVENT SERVANT

ISBN 978-1-7376011-0-4

Welcome

+ INTRODUCTION

Hey Sis!
IT'S YOUR TIME!

Did you know that in this very moment, it's your season to receive God's next blessing for your life? Did you know that He's been preparing you for greater, more, and overflow? A greater anointing, a greater power, a greater authority, a greater revelation. That's why you've been experiencing so much transition, under so much construction, and in so much warfare. Consider it an indication of breakthrough to come.

One thing I know about God is that He prepares in us what He's preparing for us. Let me say that in another way—God is already developing you for your next opportunity. He's getting you ready for the blessing He's orchestrated for your life. This is important for you to know. Why? Because you have an enemy. That enemy wants nothing more than to distract you from knowing your real power and position with God. And sis, let me tell you, your power is found in knowing God's word and praying it back to Him. That's why I created this Memory Verse and Prayer journal. I want to see all of God's daughters, my sisters in the faith, taking their power back and walking with their God-given authority.

This Memory Verse and Prayer (MVP) Journal

is a place to know, commit to memory, and apply the written word of God to your prayers and declarations. Consider this journal your shed/workshop where you sharpen this weapon of your faith and prepare to win every battle that presents itself to you.

THE WORD OF GOD IS ALIVE AND EFFECTIVE AND SHARPER THAN ANY TWO-EDGED SWORD

(Hebrews 4:12a).

IT WILL NEVER RETURN TO GOD VOID; IT WILL ALWAYS ACCOMPLISH WHAT HE SENT IT OUT TO DO

(Isaiah 55:11).

Putting His words in your mouth and letting it flow as a confession of your faith is a power move and ensures your victory in any given situation—no matter what it looks like. With that in mind, sis, let's get to knowing this word and making it a part of your daily language.

Stay Fervent,

Darlyshia A. Menzie

ABOUT THE AUTHOR

Darlyshia A. Menzie

DARLYSHIA A. MENZIE IS A KINGDOM & MARKETPLACE ENTREPRENEUR WHO TEACHES PEOPLE HOW TO GET EXCITED ABOUT THEIR LIVES BY INVESTIGATING AND INVESTING IN THEIR PERSONAL AND SPIRITUAL GROWTH.

Darlyshia is the Owner and CEO of **Fervent Servant LLC**, a coaching and consulting business whose mission is to get people excited about their lives! As a dynamic Transformational Public Speaker, Certified Life Coach, Author, Podcast Host, and Project Consultant, Darlyshia excels in charging the atmosphere with expectation and zeal! She believes that growth only happens with intention and an honest assessment of self. With that in mind, she empowers others to take responsibility for their lives and do what's necessary to live with purpose every single day! Darlyshia started her business with a desire and personal responsibility to become who she needed in different stages of her life - making her a true Fervent Servant.

HER MOTTO IS:

"Live with Intention. Serve with Passion."

It Is *Written*

SCRIPTURE REFERENCE: *Hebrews 11:1*

TRANSLATION: *CSB*

In the space below, write out the verse/passage you want to commit to memory.

Now faith is the reality of what is hoped
for, the proof of what is not seen.

This scripture is meaningful to me because...

It helps me to remember that faith is a necessary component of
what I've yet to acquire. For me to want a future that I don't
have yet or can't see yet, I need to have full confidence and con-
viction in knowing that I CAN have it and live it. Faith says it's
more than an idea, it's what's possible for me. Faith sees what
my eyes in the present don't see. Faith sees what my negative
past experiences can't see. So choosing this verse reminds me to
see beyond this moment and hope for and believe for greater.

WRITE A *Prayer to God* INCORPORATING THIS VERSE.

God, you are faithful. You see what I cannot see and you know what I do not know. You're wise in all of your ways and your plans are perfect. As I grow in relationship with you God, I want to grow in faith too. I want to take you at your word and believe the impossible. I want to accept all of the perfect plans that you've prepared for me and experience the wonderful pleasures you had in mind for me, even before I was born. Some of my past experiences have had me thinking that only some things are possible for you, but your word says that all things are possible with you. With you, God. With you is where I find this possibility. So, help my unbelief and strengthen my faith, Lord. Endow me with boldness to believe your word. My NOW FAITH is creating the future that you see for me. Help me to see it clearly. Help me to obey you enough to walk in that direction. Let me experience your dreams for me as reality. Let my circumstances catch up with the faith that I have in you. Your word cannot fail, God, so show up mighty and wild with these visions you have given me for my life. In Jesus' name, amen!

DATE: *22, July, 2021*

It Is *Written*

SCRIPTURE REFERENCE: _____

TRANSLATION: _____

In the space below, write out the verse/passage you want to commit to memory.

This scripture is meaningful to me because...

WRITE A *Prayer to God* INCORPORATING THIS VERSE.

DATE: _____

It Is *Written*

SCRIPTURE REFERENCE: _____

TRANSLATION: _____

In the space below, write out the verse/passage you want to commit to memory.

This scripture is meaningful to me because...

WRITE A *Prayer to God* INCORPORATING THIS VERSE.

DATE: _____

IT IS Written

SCRIPTURE REFERENCE: _____

TRANSLATION: _____

In the space below, write out the verse/passage you want to commit to memory.

This scripture is meaningful to me because...

WRITE A *Prayer to God* INCORPORATING THIS VERSE.

DATE: _____

It Is *Written*

SCRIPTURE REFERENCE: _____

TRANSLATION: _____

In the space below, write out the verse/passage you want to commit to memory.

This scripture is meaningful to me because...

WRITE A *Prayer to God* INCORPORATING THIS VERSE.

DATE:

IT IS *Written*

SCRIPTURE REFERENCE: _____

TRANSLATION: _____

In the space below, write out the verse/passage you want to commit to memory.

This scripture is meaningful to me because ...

WRITE A *Prayer to God* INCORPORATING THIS VERSE.

DATE: _____

It Is *Written*

SCRIPTURE REFERENCE: _____

TRANSLATION: _____

In the space below, write out the verse/passage you want to commit to memory.

This scripture is meaningful to me because...

WRITE A *Prayer to God* INCORPORATING THIS VERSE.

DATE: _____

IT IS *Written*

SCRIPTURE REFERENCE: _____

TRANSLATION: _____

In the space below, write out the verse/passage you want to commit to memory.

This scripture is meaningful to me because...

WRITE A *Prayer to God*
INCORPORATING THIS VERSE.

DATE: _____

It Is *Written*

SCRIPTURE REFERENCE: _____

TRANSLATION: _____

In the space below, write out the verse/passage you want to commit to memory.

This scripture is meaningful to me because...

WRITE A *Prayer to God* INCORPORATING THIS VERSE.

DATE: _____

It Is *Written*

SCRIPTURE REFERENCE: _____

TRANSLATION: _____

In the space below, write out the verse/passage you want to commit to memory.

This scripture is meaningful to me because...

WRITE A *Prayer to God*
INCORPORATING THIS VERSE.

DATE: _____

It Is *Written*

SCRIPTURE REFERENCE: _____

TRANSLATION: _____

In the space below, write out the verse/passage you want to commit to memory.

This scripture is meaningful to me because...

WRITE A *Prayer to God* INCORPORATING THIS VERSE.

DATE: _____

It Is *Written*

SCRIPTURE REFERENCE: _____

TRANSLATION: _____

In the space below, write out the verse/passage you want to commit to memory.

This scripture is meaningful to me because...

WRITE A *Prayer to God* INCORPORATING THIS VERSE.

DATE: _____

It Is *Written*

SCRIPTURE REFERENCE: _____

TRANSLATION: _____

In the space below, write out the verse/passage you want to commit to memory.

This scripture is meaningful to me because...

WRITE A *Prayer to God* INCORPORATING THIS VERSE.

DATE: _____

It Is *Written*

SCRIPTURE REFERENCE: _____

TRANSLATION: _____

In the space below, write out the verse/passage you want to commit to memory.

This scripture is meaningful to me because...

WRITE A *Prayer to God* INCORPORATING THIS VERSE.

DATE: _____

It Is *Written*

SCRIPTURE REFERENCE: _____

TRANSLATION: _____

In the space below, write out the verse/passage you want to commit to memory.

This scripture is meaningful to me because...

WRITE A *Prayer to God* INCORPORATING THIS VERSE.

DATE: _____

It Is *Written*

SCRIPTURE REFERENCE: _____

TRANSLATION: _____

In the space below, write out the verse/passage you want to commit to memory.

This scripture is meaningful to me because...

WRITE A *Prayer to God* INCORPORATING THIS VERSE.

DATE: _____

IT IS *Written*

SCRIPTURE REFERENCE: _____

TRANSLATION: _____

In the space below, write out the verse/passage you want to commit to memory.

This scripture is meaningful to me because...

WRITE A *Prayer to God* INCORPORATING THIS VERSE.

DATE: _____

IT IS *Written*

SCRIPTURE REFERENCE: _____

TRANSLATION: _____

In the space below, write out the verse/passage you want to commit to memory.

This scripture is meaningful to me because...

WRITE A *Prayer to God* INCORPORATING THIS VERSE.

DATE: _____

IT IS *Written*

SCRIPTURE REFERENCE: _____

TRANSLATION: _____

In the space below, write out the verse/passage you want to commit to memory.

This scripture is meaningful to me because...

WRITE A *Prayer to God* INCORPORATING THIS VERSE.

DATE: _____

It Is *Written*

SCRIPTURE REFERENCE: _____

TRANSLATION: _____

In the space below, write out the verse/passage you want to commit to memory.

This scripture is meaningful to me because...

WRITE A *Prayer to God* INCORPORATING THIS VERSE.

DATE: _____

IT IS *Written*

SCRIPTURE REFERENCE: _____

TRANSLATION: _____

In the space below, write out the verse/passage you want to commit to memory.

This scripture is meaningful to me because...

WRITE A *Prayer to God* INCORPORATING THIS VERSE.

DATE: _____

IT IS *Written*

SCRIPTURE REFERENCE: _____

TRANSLATION: _____

In the space below, write out the verse/passage you want to commit to memory.

This scripture is meaningful to me because...

WRITE A *Prayer to God* INCORPORATING THIS VERSE.

DATE: _____

It Is *Written*

SCRIPTURE REFERENCE: _____

TRANSLATION: _____

In the space below, write out the verse/passage you want to commit to memory.

This scripture is meaningful to me because...

WRITE A *Prayer to God* INCORPORATING THIS VERSE.

DATE: _____

IT IS *Written*

SCRIPTURE REFERENCE: _____

TRANSLATION: _____

In the space below, write out the verse/passage you want to commit to memory.

This scripture is meaningful to me because...

WRITE A *Prayer to God* INCORPORATING THIS VERSE.

DATE: _____

IT IS *Written*

SCRIPTURE REFERENCE: _____

TRANSLATION: _____

In the space below, write out the verse/passage you want to commit to memory.

This scripture is meaningful to me because...

WRITE A *Prayer to God* INCORPORATING THIS VERSE.

DATE: _____

IT IS Written

SCRIPTURE REFERENCE: _____

TRANSLATION: _____

In the space below, write out the verse/passage you want to commit to memory.

This scripture is meaningful to me because...

WRITE A *Prayer to God* INCORPORATING THIS VERSE.

DATE: _____

It Is *Written*

SCRIPTURE REFERENCE: _____

TRANSLATION: _____

In the space below, write out the verse/passage you want to commit to memory.

This scripture is meaningful to me because...

WRITE A *Prayer to God* INCORPORATING THIS VERSE.

DATE: _____

IT IS *Written*

SCRIPTURE REFERENCE: _____

TRANSLATION: _____

In the space below, write out the verse/passage you want to commit to memory.

This scripture is meaningful to me because...

WRITE A *Prayer to God* INCORPORATING THIS VERSE.

DATE: _____

It Is *Written*

SCRIPTURE REFERENCE: _____

TRANSLATION: _____

In the space below, write out the verse/passage you want to commit to memory.

This scripture is meaningful to me because...

WRITE A *Prayer to God* INCORPORATING THIS VERSE.

DATE: _____

It Is *Written*

SCRIPTURE REFERENCE: _____

TRANSLATION: _____

In the space below, write out the verse/passage you want to commit to memory.

This scripture is meaningful to me because...

WRITE A *Prayer to God* INCORPORATING THIS VERSE.

DATE: _____

IT IS *Written*

SCRIPTURE REFERENCE: _____

TRANSLATION: _____

In the space below, write out the verse/passage you want to commit to memory.

This scripture is meaningful to me because...

WRITE A *Prayer to God* INCORPORATING THIS VERSE.

DATE: _____

It Is *Written*

SCRIPTURE REFERENCE: _____

TRANSLATION: _____

In the space below, write out the verse/passage you want to commit to memory.

This scripture is meaningful to me because...

WRITE A *Prayer to God* INCORPORATING THIS VERSE.

DATE: _____

IT IS *Written*

SCRIPTURE REFERENCE: _____

TRANSLATION: _____

In the space below, write out the verse/passage you want to commit to memory.

This scripture is meaningful to me because...

WRITE A *Prayer to God* INCORPORATING THIS VERSE.

DATE: _____

It Is *Written*

SCRIPTURE REFERENCE: _____

TRANSLATION: _____

In the space below, write out the verse/passage you want to commit to memory.

This scripture is meaningful to me because...

WRITE A *Prayer to God* INCORPORATING THIS VERSE.

DATE: _____

IT IS *Written*

SCRIPTURE REFERENCE: _____

TRANSLATION: _____

In the space below, write out the verse/passage you want to commit to memory.

This scripture is meaningful to me because...

WRITE A *Prayer to God* INCORPORATING THIS VERSE.

DATE: _____

IT IS *Written*

SCRIPTURE REFERENCE: _____

TRANSLATION: _____

In the space below, write out the verse/passage you want to commit to memory.

This scripture is meaningful to me because...

WRITE A *Prayer to God* INCORPORATING THIS VERSE.

DATE: _____

IT IS *Written*

SCRIPTURE REFERENCE: _____

TRANSLATION: _____

In the space below, write out the verse/passage you want to commit to memory.

This scripture is meaningful to me because...

WRITE A *Prayer to God* INCORPORATING THIS VERSE.

DATE: _____

IT IS *Written*

SCRIPTURE REFERENCE: _____

TRANSLATION: _____

In the space below, write out the verse/passage you want to commit to memory.

This scripture is meaningful to me because...

WRITE A *Prayer to God* INCORPORATING THIS VERSE.

DATE: _____

IT IS *Written*

SCRIPTURE REFERENCE: _____

TRANSLATION: _____

In the space below, write out the verse/passage you want to commit to memory.

This scripture is meaningful to me because...

WRITE A *Prayer to God* INCORPORATING THIS VERSE.

DATE: _____

It Is *Written*

SCRIPTURE REFERENCE: _____

TRANSLATION: _____

In the space below, write out the verse/passage you want to commit to memory.

This scripture is meaningful to me because...

WRITE A *Prayer to God* INCORPORATING THIS VERSE.

DATE: _____

It Is *Written*

SCRIPTURE REFERENCE: _____

TRANSLATION: _____

In the space below, write out the verse/passage you want to commit to memory.

This scripture is meaningful to me because...

WRITE A *Prayer to God*
INCORPORATING THIS VERSE.

DATE: _____

IT IS *Written*

SCRIPTURE REFERENCE: _____

TRANSLATION: _____

In the space below, write out the verse/passage you want to commit to memory.

This scripture is meaningful to me because...

WRITE A *Prayer to God* INCORPORATING THIS VERSE.

DATE: _____

It Is *Written*

SCRIPTURE REFERENCE: _____

TRANSLATION: _____

In the space below, write out the verse/passage you want to commit to memory.

This scripture is meaningful to me because...

WRITE A *Prayer to God* INCORPORATING THIS VERSE.

DATE: _____

IT IS *Written*

SCRIPTURE REFERENCE: _____

TRANSLATION: _____

In the space below, write out the verse/passage you want to commit to memory.

This scripture is meaningful to me because...

WRITE A *Prayer to God* INCORPORATING THIS VERSE.

DATE: _____

It Is *Written*

SCRIPTURE REFERENCE: _____

TRANSLATION: _____

In the space below, write out the verse/passage you want to commit to memory.

This scripture is meaningful to me because...

WRITE A *Prayer to God* INCORPORATING THIS VERSE.

DATE: _____

IT IS *Written*

SCRIPTURE REFERENCE: _____

TRANSLATION: _____

In the space below, write out the verse/passage you want to commit to memory.

This scripture is meaningful to me because...

WRITE A *Prayer to God* INCORPORATING THIS VERSE.

DATE: _____

It Is *Written*

SCRIPTURE REFERENCE: _____

TRANSLATION: _____

In the space below, write out the verse/passage you want to commit to memory.

This scripture is meaningful to me because...

WRITE A *Prayer to God* INCORPORATING THIS VERSE.

DATE: _____

IT IS *Written*

SCRIPTURE REFERENCE: _____

TRANSLATION: _____

In the space below, write out the verse/passage you want to commit to memory.

This scripture is meaningful to me because...

WRITE A *Prayer to God* INCORPORATING THIS VERSE.

DATE: _____

IT IS *Written*

SCRIPTURE REFERENCE: _____

TRANSLATION: _____

In the space below, write out the verse/passage you want to commit to memory.

This scripture is meaningful to me because...

WRITE A *Prayer to God* INCORPORATING THIS VERSE.

DATE: _____

It Is *Written*

SCRIPTURE REFERENCE: _____

TRANSLATION: _____

In the space below, write out the verse/passage you want to commit to memory.

This scripture is meaningful to me because...

WRITE A *Prayer to God* INCORPORATING THIS VERSE.

DATE: _____

It Is *Written*

SCRIPTURE REFERENCE: _____

TRANSLATION: _____

In the space below, write out the verse/passage you want to commit to memory.

This scripture is meaningful to me because...

WRITE A *Prayer to God* INCORPORATING THIS VERSE.

DATE: _____

It Is *Written*

SCRIPTURE REFERENCE: _____

TRANSLATION: _____

In the space below, write out the verse/passage you want to commit to memory.

This scripture is meaningful to me because...

WRITE A *Prayer to God* INCORPORATING THIS VERSE.

DATE: _____

It Is *Written*

SCRIPTURE REFERENCE: _____

TRANSLATION: _____

In the space below, write out the verse/passage you want to commit to memory.

This scripture is meaningful to me because...

WRITE A *Prayer to God* INCORPORATING THIS VERSE.

DATE: _____

IT IS *Written*

SCRIPTURE REFERENCE: _____

TRANSLATION: _____

In the space below, write out the verse/passage you want to commit to memory.

This scripture is meaningful to me because...

WRITE A *Prayer to God* INCORPORATING THIS VERSE.

DATE: _____

It Is *Written*

SCRIPTURE REFERENCE: _____

TRANSLATION: _____

In the space below, write out the verse/passage you want to commit to memory.

This scripture is meaningful to me because...

WRITE A *Prayer to God* INCORPORATING THIS VERSE.

DATE: _____

It Is *Written*

SCRIPTURE REFERENCE: _____

TRANSLATION: _____

In the space below, write out the verse/passage you want to commit to memory.

This scripture is meaningful to me because...

WRITE A *Prayer to God* INCORPORATING THIS VERSE.

DATE: _____

It Is *Written*

SCRIPTURE REFERENCE: _____

TRANSLATION: _____

In the space below, write out the verse/passage you want to commit to memory.

This scripture is meaningful to me because...

WRITE A *Prayer to God* INCORPORATING THIS VERSE.

DATE: _____

Darlyshia's
PUBLISHED WORKS

AT THE END OF ME:
A Journey of Self-Esteem and Identity

FACE TO FACE WITH ME:
Power Questions To Ask Yourself

BE L.I.G.H.T.:
A Mindset Shift From the Mundane To The Miraculous

Awaken, Oh Dreamer *Dreamer's Journal*

Pray, Don't Prey Intercession *Journal*

A Prophetic Word Prophecy *Journal*

To learn more about Darlyshia, make a purchase, connect for an event/project, or join her groups/courses, visit
WWW.DARLYSHIAMENZIE.COM

CPSIA information can be obtained
at www.ICGtesting.com
Printed in the USA
JSHW040108310821
18300JS00003B/27

9 781737 601104